ANOTHER I

www.shadyhallab.com/anotheri

ISBN: 978-0-9951546-2-9

ANOTHER I

A Collection of Poetry and Prose

SHADY HALLAB

*To those who once caused joy, hate, love and pain.
I wouldn't have written this book without you.*

ACKNOWLEDGEMENTS

I would like to express my appreciation to the many people who saw me through this book; to all those who provided support, read, wrote, offered comments, and assisted in the editing, proofreading and design.

Above all I want to thank my wife, Suleen, who supported and encouraged me in spite of the long journey.

I would like to thank the talented Ammar Bey for the creative art work. Thank you original Karim Zock for all the time and effort placed in designing the book cover and interior. I would like to thank also Hassan Talliss and Dima Faris for helping me in the process of selection and editing.

A big shout goes to the Blurb team who made publishing this book possible.

– Part I –
Love

Sunflower

The curtains went down,
And claps echoed the theater of the town.
It was a far-away little village
Where rain never stopped.
People would go out tonight,
All holding umbrellas and lights.
There was a little girl,
Who opted to dance under these rainy clouds –
She would get all wet,
But she wouldn't feel her sweat.
Her name was sunflower,
And her sun was a smile that never set.
This little girl is a grown up now,
And she meets a guy
Who never went off the train.
She called him, wind.
He was always away,
Distant from her dance,
Close enough though like her star.
She would see him in every drop of her rain –
But the silence took her music away.
Dancing under the rain felt alone, on her own,
And the wind just never came.
The train never had a stop back –
Her sun had to set this time,
But only to allow time to flip on –
The world will rise,
And the curtains will open back.
The show will run,
And they are holding hands.
The wind is back,
The music turns a vibe on;
Flowers open up...
She smiles.
She flames.
The wing,
Stays.

A Queen

Oversees,
Behind the line of blue horizon,
The golden cloudy sparks –
The place where love survives.
A blossom of a white sprinkle
Keeps blowing my mind in –
Taking my time away,
Leaving me out,
And layering the sears in shape.
A blue hear made white,
And all white shears only red.
The color of viding tocks –
Clipping all mocks,
Make all men swore.
She was suing her lean,
Not knowing that she is simply a queen.
Feel.

My Tender One

I open up my eyes,
And vague as it seems,
I couldn't find any secrets tonight.
Everything around hesitated,
Except for the sun.
Her golden hair makes the sunrays
Fade away shy.
The beauty of her eyes
Makes the words silent to describe.
She was too much for
A little bit of charm.
The force in her softness,
And the happiness in her sadness
Made me open my eyes to dream of her smile.
Her skin is a passion by itself,
She was stunning white,
And I couldn't hold myself.
She attracts the beauty of life.
She was all by herself,
And the world turns into
A tender light by her side.
She wasn't someone that I've met before,
And it made me think –
Fight in my mind, twice.
I turn to writing,
But silence can't write.
Words flying all over my sky
Shattered,
Million times.

Between Worlds

I read your words,
And I flew between worlds.
I scratched the wall for hours -
At night screaming the sound –
Of a dead coming back to life.
Someone who came again but
With no eyes to see light or dark.
He is here not to live through
But to feel life.
Time took the bright out of his shine,
And his color wouldn't come back
Unless he scrolls his fingers
And touch.

Childhood Rush

I find you in a place,
Where there was no space.
Time was all yours,
And I was just a second in your night.
A frozen tick tock for your clock –
I persist and refuse to let go.
You dance around,
And I don't move an eye –
You whisper in my ears secrets of time;
And I tell you that you became
My line of a shine.
The flow settles at your smile,
And I grabbed your hands
As if I were taking what is mine.
Your intelligence disguised in your innocence,
And my Evil revived at your night.
You took away all the nights,
And left me surrounded by suns.
You want me to wake up,
But I insist,
I persist.
You shall live the dream of mine...
We'll make it a secret of a childhood rush...
And we'll give that frozen second a cool-off.
Live a dream, close your eyes.
Make them mine.

Paradise of Lies

In a shining night,
Darkness fought against light
Dreams had to face screams,
And nightmares were in teams.
The devil was dancing,
They played with hands,
They touched, kissed,
And he had her for the night,
They stole my moonlight,
It was meant –
They won their lives.
Hell turned into paradise of lies.
Tears cracked out of my eyes,
One after another - all celebrating life.
Sun rises at five in the morning,
And I step up.
I was very tired and stressed all night.
I didn't know why, but I felt it inside.
I knew it all, but I lied.
I preferred to disguise the truth,
Into a wonderful lie.
Oh that night,
She sold my world for her life,
What life?
The music was gone,
The lights blew up,
And here's myself –
A silent I.

My Every Star

My story starts with a lie;
A lie of denying a smile.
I haven't been gone,
And she has never been far.
I leave the sun,
And I find her in every star.
I tell the world that she's gone,
But I fake my dancing like a star.
My world is moving on,
But I remain seated on that same bar –
Thinking of how to get her out of my mind.
With all the braveness that I've got –
She still captures my heart.
I can't describe to her,
I am her little secret, even if she denies –
And I crave to continue in this lie.
She will be the queen of someone far,
And I'll live in a rebuff.
She won't be mine,
But I belong to her by heart.
It doesn't take a thousand memories to fall;
Her single smile might be enough.
She had found something in my eyes,
I knew it each time she smiled.
Don't hide – you're my every star.

Forbidden

You danced with a sparkling eye,
And you flipped my world –
Like when throwing a dice.
I knew that our dance was forbidden,
Yet I couldn't resist the eye.
You told me that we could never exist,
And I shut you down.
A silent kiss that could never lie.
You had told me that we could not touch,
And I asked you to just give up.
You asked me to wake up,
And I invited you to join the dream of mine –
It will always remain as long as you don't mind –
We can never be,
Unless only in our minds.
You've been missing being with the one,
And I traveled the world searching for that one.
Fate makes fun of faith,
And grants us a story –
That can't even start.
This is my story with you,
An empty book –
A colorful cover and a happy title.
I creed for you to become just mine,
And give me a truth that can never lie.
I couldn't hide –
Show me your eyes.
We can't just drop,
We will never be,
But we are.

Eternal, in Mind

I turned off all lights,
And I had one candle of yours by my side –
The flame of our shine is on...
Words couldn't get out,
But my beat wouldn't stop.
I can hear your voice deep inside –
You are far enough to just hide
Take out the sun,
And draw a moon in the shape of a smile –
Come here;
We'll have one single star.
I'll keep you between my arms,
And you'll just close your eyes –
While pointing out up high...
We'll go where we'll belong,
The sky is where we may start.
Time will rise by our side.
Shorten my long nights,
The sunrise is our stop.
You'll smile –
I'll know that the world is fine...
You ask me if life would to ever change me,
And I answer back with a lie...
We'll change life...
You wonder about the truth,
And I come back to you
With us –
We are the truth.
The one light that cannot go off;
A flame, just like the one by my side –
Eternal, in mind.

Shadows of Sun

The clock didn't tick.
It simply stopped;
The world spins around in hidden eyes.
The breathing doesn't stop,
And it pumps life to survive.
I freeze there in your eyes.
The stars don't look like it is night,
And the sun sets a time out.
A small place is what we've got.
The remainder is what we all want –
A kiss never seemed like one,
And my other I didn't want to stop.
The wild storm inside wanted to come out –
Life brought my brain to plug.
I am still waiting for the sun to hide,
So I return to where I found my one.
I'll look at you, and you'll be shy.
You would want to tell me something,
And I would just make you smile,
Allow you to go alive –
Peace in and war out.
Fear the sun and wish for dark.
Eternal I will keep your eyes closed.
Wake up one day by my side –
Make out a dream immortal.
We'll watch the sun come out.
The ocean will color blue,
And my little window will become our eyes.
I'll show you a beautiful lie,
And I'll teach you how silence can talk.
I'll give you peace if you do not like –
I'll spin the globe in your arms –
Just smile.

On Her Side

A lonely star up in the sky did not want to fly –
Somewhere she was the queen,
She found pleasure in losing sight;
And I was just a rhyme.
She had to sing all night long –
Enjoyed a touch of another one;
It woke the death out of me,
Took my breathing out of my chest –
Broke the lights, burned the hell down –
Death came inside out,
I've lost, and I wanted to tell the whole world –
About innocence that found a way out.
Blood pressured the pain,
And the pain fled into the soul –
Ones thought they were going up –
Ended up at upside down
Paradise fell down to hell:
Liars were brought up –
Goodness became a fantasy,
And the world stroke a madness –
She was a liar with a kind heart –
One among all that excluded my I.
World, why?
Lies, lies, lies.
A world made out of a big lie.
She was not a stranger God,
But made a visit to the other side.
It was a place where one can buy a night –
And sell away lifetime.
She discovered the pleasure of darkness,
And unleashed the reality of happiness.
This inner mind was stuck on his side;
Retain yourself to the master of yourself,
Care enough to raise those sins inside –
Become the king of your own night.
It all drills down to lies,
Oh of these she had a lot.
Blame her and then realize –
It's all what she has ever got.

Blue Sight

Twinkling around my fingers,
My pen was longing to take my sorrow out.
It is the same pen
That glew out of happiness many times,
Around the fingers
That were kissed by my one,
Tonight I remember her light –
She had a shining smile.
For a while I couldn't remember
Any of that at all;
But I'm alive –
Lots of pain covered up time,
And I tried to run away.
I was destined to hold a pen.
I dismissed my blue and all light –
And I uncovered a moon
To become my biggest lie.
I learned that her eyes revealed my path –
An ultimate ride towards a truth
That always denies;
A reality of inexistence of our night.
A dead kiss that awakened me up.
A departing love that can't stand –
I had to come back alive.
The moon is destined to seek my sight,
A sky will always clear up,
And I will continue to write.

Blind Spot

Deep somewhere far,
It was really dark.
I was running after my life;
It was absent,
But the moon spread light.
I still feel that touch.
It was kind and tough;
It made me stranger to my own life.
It took a second for a star to show up.
Even the moon appeared shy,
And darkness was silent –
But sparkled a smile.
For once, my time just stopped –
This lonely tear couldn't drop.
Scary if it stops;
But the story could go off.
Fear is not far,
And time is now ordered to run.
A tear has to float away the eye;
Darkness will come back to its own self –
As angry as it can be;
It is the reality that I did not draw –
A path that I was put on;
Time is a machine;
Even if I cannot believe –
But she was my relief.
I turned blind,
And I went on with screams.
The truth is silent though –
But I wanted to be seen.
Death wants to blow souls away,
And I wanted death to come –
So I can take him away.
I wanted to relieve him out of my life,
And to replace him with her –
Eternal me tonight.

Reborn in You

I have a dream that is about to seize;
Build a house with no walls,
Live in the middle of the crowd,
Enjoy the rain out plain –
And you're my only loud.
Drive the way on our own,
Make love till we're reborn,
Live on your eyes –
Till ours blind as one.
Steal a path and call it flat;
Make it ours and just run.
Leave on a wave of light,
And don't ask me to come back-
We will be gone.
Somewhere reality becomes a dream
And the dream is an image of ours –
Colors that would make you fly.
Wake your beat up,
Listen to my eyes,
And find your words close to the heart –
Think of me and remember,
I am one love that brought you alive.

Betray Me

It was the first time.
The hand shook,
And the pen fell,
A tear flew down,
Toward a big star.
I woke up,
I looked in the mirror
I saw myself blind.
Light filled my eyes,
But nothing I could see,
Except the dark.
He wanted to betray
And run away.
It was another lie
He never met a truth.
I lost words,
Precious feelings.
I gave up.
He lived in me.
I never thought of him.
He the white became my black.
And I, colors in the sky,
Turned to be hollow in dark.
One last night with a sun
And the moon shone.
It made sense,
It didn't. He never asked.
Yet I never stopped.
Life loses sight
I sustain. And the passion for more
Never calms down.
He wants to leave, and I want to run away.
We both leave each other.
We wake up on the same star.
Tears won't do this time.
He wants to stay in me.
I do not want to beat
Anymore. He is I and I am not him.
The story never ends, But it continues till a
Start.

Pass

Here I come;
The world was not waiting,
But I was rushing.
I thought it had to have me,
But it didn't even notice me.
I wake up,
Then I dream.
I walk, and I talk –
So I live, but no one believes.
Dusty as it might seem.
You escape somewhere –
Colors you can see.
Few days pass –
A world moving fast,
I am stuck in between.
I look at the clock,
And it never stops.
My world is moving,
But I am affixed to
Someone that I am.
I cannot stay.
Come with me,
Somewhere we can be.

Diverge

The story starts at an end,
And the end never comes.
My words did not stand,
And my heart reached out.
My never became an ever,
And a strike of faith
Brought me back.
Silence is her king –
As we travel in time.
I would dazzle her with lies –
And she would shine up to a truth,
An unparalleled story
That had no symmetry.
We hold hands,
And the future comes
Into a split of time –
The past fades hard,
And those words of hers
Finally got out.
It was what she had
Forbidden by heart –
Rayon of thoughts
Enlightened our spot.
My world did not halt,
And it did not run.
It just felt alive –
Strive.

The End

Thousands of questions start with an answer,
And many of the lonely nights are crowded –
With people we can't remember
Who they really are.
This is the story of every story-teller,
He takes you with words
And brings you back with lies.
Listen to the sound of innocent eyes;
Doesn't it make you wonder
About the secret behind smiles?
You poisoned me with a thousand dreams –
And you would never stop by.
Roll the story over, and let the world watch.
A shy look hides a lot,
But it reveals as much as it hides –
I did not want to tell you much,
And you did not want to listen at all.
You wanted to play hard,
And I am never easy at the start.
Chances are granted by heart.
The hero is not you –
But at every question,
I could have had you on mind.
Still, the night deepens in dark.
I look at a star, which has given up my eyes.
Then I call up high, 'give me a sign'.
Don't look outside,
Trust your eyes for what you do not see –
Discover the reality of her scene;
Behind every word, there's a story,
And for every story there's a hero.
You take my words, and you chose the hero.
Give a chance a fair story to tell.
One day you tell someone –
I had a hero and I chose the end.

Who You Are

Got inside the mirror –
I became the other side of life.
I looked at my eyes, and I couldn't lie.
I wanted to tell you,
But silence kept it all.
I came back in time,
And I didn't know why.
I never left;
Yet you weren't here at all.
Even my words struggled a lot.
I freeze, and you smile.
I stand far away,
And you wave at me with a goodbye.
I thought that I was gone,
But you never appeared nearby.
I asked you to close your eyes,
And you refused to turn off the lights.
I woke up from a beautiful dream,
And someone invited me by –
It wasn't you.
Where were you?
Neither in paradise nor in hell had I found you.
You are very close that I can't see you.
Your screams are very loud –
High to a point that I can't hear you.
I never had your words, and I blame life.
Reveal yourself –
I observe the horizon going away,
And I see nothing, I feel nothing.
You show up asking me why?
I stay up, and I betray life.
I lie, and to you I smile.
The question is sacred,
But I still dare to ask.
You say forget,
And I wish.
You say leave,
And I can't die.
You say sleep,
And I dream.
You and I,

How beautiful may it seem.
Look around,
You don't see many –
There are few ones.
So I ask,
If we ever were one,
Would you survive?
Come into my mirror –
The answer is one,
Yet you may not be my one.
Believe it or not;
My mirror is my other I.

Railroads

From within the middle of a crowd,
I, among others, am craving to pass time.
Through the rush of beating hearts,
And under the same moon that
I used to talk with all the time.
My reflection becomes hollow –
And my world becomes one spot.
I stop moving, and I cannot walk.
It paralyzes me non-stop –
I focus to feel touched;
Rain is all what I got.
I arrive at where I always wanted to get –
I find a train,
Remember the train my one?
It is coming;
Life is beating inside –
Blood is pumping so tough.
Doors open, and no one inside.
I seek where I always run –
Where are you hun?
World runs fast –
She is upfront, and I am rolling back.
For two worlds that cannot intersect,
I will never turn around.

Departure of Love

And, who is she?
It is her who brought
Joy to my life, and
Happiness that drove my heart.
We, me and her, embraced love,
Whispered during many nights,
And created our own bubble –
Of silence inside a loud warm fight.
Still every time we touch,
This fire burns up.
We always had long nights,
Our hearts would beat in time –
We would beat all night.
The sun comes out,
And she moves on.
Once upon a time, she was.
She is trapped behind –
I was on time, but she was not.
Alone is what we have.
Who moved on?
We both did –
So we meet again another time.

Be Mine

With the coming of each night,
My mind betrays my heart...
And my thinking brings another one...
I don't know who you are anymore.
There's something inside me there.
It stretches my words to touch your heart.
You, I never meant to talk about you,
But my heart keeps insisting on you.
I need to tell you something,
But I am afraid to lose everything...
It's not that I am not sure,
It's just life that stole my stars.
Will you survive?
I can't stay in darkness anymore,
I need to sin by the truth of my heart
You need to know who you are,
And tell me that you're just mine.
You cannot play my patience;
It has eaten me since distance took part.
We don't admit that we could become one –
But we both have tonight.
Give it a try –

Prisoner

The dawn is near,
But the cage is sealed.
Someone is falling free –
In his own locker breed.
I see others swing;
Please let me get out of my fringe.
People swing.
I am turning around myself.
Let me sit with you once
For one night.
I won't be the same.
I promise if you may
I am telling you
I won't be the same.
Even if someone has to blame,
And you see me packing
Can't stay anymore.
I am leaving.
Come with me.
You know the way.
Light up the path,
Open up my thinking.
Smiles, Smiles, Smiles
That's all what I'm seeing.
Sun came into my world.
But I am locked up,
Don't you remember?
Locked up free.

Safe

The lights were soft,
A red candle kept our corner up –
A mirror facing me from behind,
And you were scratching the wall –
Inside out.
I saw it all in your eyes,
But no words came out.
The clock docks,
It becomes midnight.
I bring you by the hand,
You seemed scared.
I whisper in your ear:
'Close your eyes'
You take my hand,
And put it to sense your heart.
There was no beat,
It can't just stop.
I took it back.
I get closer into your eyes,
All the love in the world was hidden inside;
Silent and calm.
The candle goes off.
I cover you with my arms.
'Don't move'
But you wanted to touch.
Trembling lips became mine.
We both froze in time;
As if the earth paused,
It couldn't spin around.
We spelled life out,
And we gave the dream a night
Sleep my love,
There will be no waking up.
Lie.

– Part II –
Life

Until It Rhymes

I've been trying to write,
But I still can't find a start.
I am flying high in the sky;
Somewhere I can't even find myself.
The height shattered me into pieces.
Those pieces do not combine.
I listen to myself and I don't rhyme.
This music is really loud,
It gets into my mind.
Hundreds of ideas,
It is tearing me apart.
I grew old in mind –
That I can barely slow to catch up.
I cannot change the world, but I can try.
Regret is not for losing a battle,
But rather for not fighting one.
Opportunity is what many of us –
Get in between times.
The loss is when we run away from a chance.
We hide behind the moment
And blame the surprise.
We become too lazy to fight.
This sweet old-day success
Paralyzes you inside-out.
It is like winning a marathon,
You feel blessed but yet so pressured to sustain.
Your fear, driven by your success,
Grows day after day
Making you unable to run.
The winner becomes paralyzed.
He can't even walk.
He needs support to go on,
Yet the bar is set high.
Deep inside, success is killing,
But your attitude is who you are.
Something inside that strives to fight,
Even to beat in against your own self.
An end has no point;
And you do not know whether there was a start.
It is more like a state of mind.
Somewhere really far but born along
As if programmed to reach the sky.

A Few can't handle heights.
We all have one shot.
Somebody who can't fly –
May try to pull you off.
Then, no matter how high you are –
You're going down.
Trust is when you are able to –
Find who can protect you in tough times.
Many of these are tough ones.
The easy becomes scarce these times.
Some of us have already found shortcuts –
Pity them as it detains them –
Till easy becomes too difficult to survive.
Then a paradise turns into a painful truth.
You wouldn't know what you want.
You become someone strange to the dreams –
That made the person who you really are.
Fight, fight, till a time when your peaceful song really rhymes.

Bright

Midnight clocks,
And I knock all the lights off –
A blink of memories thrives,
The world comes back around –
I shake a bit and hold myself tight.
The story of the ocean,
The cold feet,
And the late night.
The sun comes up,
And I am straddling zones in and others out.
I break down,
But I keep repeating to myself not.
Think, twice.
Beat the memories with smiles.
The world can't come back –
You would need to go upfront,
Meet the future.
Divorce from the past –
Commit to the present.
And the clock docks –
It keeps telling me
What I can't tell anyone else –
'Time has already passed'
The circle has no gaps,
And we run around –
Searching for ourselves.
Sustain till you remain –
Otherwise,
Just sight.
Prospect,
Go bright.

Free Soul

Undress a thought,
Walk to the other side.
Senseless you will become,
Meanwhile freely alive.
Many words won't make up to a lot.
Still colorful, ones you've got.
You play your destiny.
I won't ask you to talk –
It is done.
Close your eyes –
Travel through the night.
Leave my life,
Happiness shall shine.
Your words will stop,
Silence what you always loved –
Control, not.
Leave it to the heart.
Tell them –
It is a start.

Let Me Begin

Diary, you have been so dear to me –
That I left you all blank.
You tell a story of my start,
And with a lot of creativity,
You draw an end.
I thought that I had to bring the best out of you,
But you had it all.
Filled with empty pages is what you are.
I read with fascination,
I did not know that I had risen so high –
I never imagined that I would just drop.
These blurry stars, now I understand.
You tricked me with that cover –
And now, it is me who needs a cover.
How can a diary give up on its hero?
Am I the one, or an anyone?
But I traveled and fought –
You thought I was running away
Violence is all what I have spread.
Reality is that I was searching –
For my lines in your pages.
Now that I found you,
I do not understand the end –
And the beginning is not where I am.
What do you crave in me?
I am obsessed in writing –
I'll finish you, tonight.
But if you want –
Take me in, I won't write.
Peaceful I promise to become
Just as white as you are,
I come with peace.
Trust me,
You're my diary.

Shot Down

Fake those ties –
Attach to an illusion
Made of beautiful lies –
Drag yourself somewhere far
To a place where
No one would believe you anymore
Build a home there,
So no one would visit.
Live up into closed doors,
And don't keep a bell.
Fence your gate,
Protect your darkness.
Lord your fate –
And scare happiness away.
Bully yourself till you quit,
And dismiss your mind.
Fall somewhere you can't come back –
And put a joy into suffering.
Endless loneliness –
And a dark heart
Brings the worst in you –
And that's who you really are.
Do not try.

Alive

Tears were mine.
Clouds acted fright.
Wind was stuck.
Breathing I stopped.
Moon was dark.
Fake was this night.
Dim my stars!
As I closed my eyes.
Path I never took –
Is waiting for me to look.
Why to lie?
I am a spirit,
A mandated one.
Regret?
Brave you are.
Write your pain out.
Revenge a sun within.
Laugh really loud.
Scare the death away.
It will not stop,
Pop more time.
Otherwise, you are behind.
Far that time surpasses you.
Taken over that night –
Why to survive?
You are assumed alive.
Reality is blind –
Celebrate mortality with me;
It makes you cherish life.
An illusion in my mind –
Welcome to your reality.
Explore me.
I am a nearby –
Your own end –
Of a long dream –
That will be shuttered apart.
Where is the Lord in my faith?
No one is answering my calls.
Am I there yet?
Deny. Lie.

She's Waiting

In a world made out of her mind,
The little girl grew up and never aged.
Life taught her how to act big –
Even though she never wanted to dig.
But she had to blink –
Took the train so little
The doors closed,
And never opened
Till her station arrived.
She was ready for her stop –
To get off. Leave. Disappear.
She took the ride with an innocent smile,
Greeted her stop with a fake laugh.
Back then, she got on with a surprise,
And now she is back normalized;
Disciplined to treat life.
Rules, of these she learned a lot.
Freedom became of a price –
Money made it all at a discount.
The valuable of all time is already gone,
And her age yet to witness more of that time.
Patience is manner to pass time –
She will wait,
Till she is gone.

The Initial Realm

Little sparks take the night inside the sun,
And the world flowers yellow around –
A little green vegetal grows a color,
Tears down the uniform and slips in a warren.
The tunnel is long, but all has an end.
Except for life, colorful, it has to sun.
Humans, greedy ones, blare for more –
Even through the needy ones.
The essence is innocent,
Guild is men-fabrique.
They would paint out playful lines,
Watercolors that fade away at night;
When the clouds drop the rain,
And wash away the fake marks...
Only the truth stays, like a scar.
Spiritual templates, faithless buildings –
Reality is in the heart.
World,
Come back –
To the initial realm.

Dry

I was stuck inside myself,
Trying to call someone,
Unable to hear myself.
I was left behind –
In a second of strike;
It felt like I was shot,
As if my soul was going out,
And I couldn't even speak up.
It seemed more like a tear
That couldn't find an eye –
So it was stuck deep inside.
I entered a whole new world,
Full of a single lie.
I was severely wounded –
Yet I was the enemy,
And they were the allies.
Fighting for tomorrow,
I was shot before it arrived.
Both shot me down,
And I couldn't call anyone.
I had no one.
Trembling, draining, bleeding –
I had to stay silent, become silence.
I had to die in peace, to survive.

One More Chance

It took few seconds to turn the lights off,
The colors faded tight,
And the world simply turned off.
I didn't know where I was or when it was.
For few seconds, I was the other second –
Everything was gone,
And the wall went down.
She packed up,
But I am the traveler this time –
The seat was waiting for me,
But I'll be standing up,
Screaming in the middle of the crowd.
Everyone else was yelling high.
I was just a guy, any guy.
My name took off,
Unknown is what we know –
Music to a depth,
A letter to an illiterate –
The challenge of a riddle,
I was and never am.
The will after my I was already gone.
And what's left?
These lousy words reviving the pain.
Flashbacks from old times –
It doesn't feel right –
Under the skin, I feel high.
How would it heal?
I close my eyes,
But it's already dark.
I couldn't stop,
And I had to push all the way up –
So I hang up.
I play time;
I get alive,
And I repeat –
One more time.

Wake Up

Lost in a dream.
The children of innocence woke up on a dream;
Each wanted to become a world of his own.
The light took each one of them away,
Somewhere darkness can't see.
They made the luck of theirs,
And they decided to write a story.
A story that was real, too real.
Each one of them had a dream,
And the years took them ahead
Of what they had seen.
The memories went black
And today, it is the dream.
Different directions,
And where have you been?
They wanted to change the world;
Did the world make them change?
They wanted to pursue the dream,
A dream about the world,
The way they saw it free.
The world spoiled them into greed.
They forgot about the world,
They got real.
Many years it has been,
And still deep,
In the heart somewhere moments
When they, actually, were the dream.
They were the hope before it had ever been,
And they were the spark before it all began.
Come back to that sleep,
Remember your dream.
Image the world the way
You believed it to be,
The way you wanted to lead,
And remember that once upon a time
The world searched for you,
Selected you, and believed in you.
Some of them lost the direction,
And forgot the essence of the scene.
Some other ones got lost in their dreams,
Lived their own dreams,

And never made it real.
Take a second out, remember,
Tour dream was about the world
And not about where you want to be.
Come back to
What have made the you out of you,
Bring out that difference in you,
And play the role of no one but your own self.
Believe.

Six Sides

Walk down the road,
Look at the tall front on the side,
A man mirrors all the way up –
Looks at himself gigantic
He smiles –
Get into the shop –
Purchase a dream of six sides.
One of it was the world,
And others, colorful, like her style.
The space gave him the pace,
And the taste was up to his say.
He blinks to pass time.
Patience was running his life –
It takes a man to hold on,
And stick to a reality
That has no dream.
It is the he who can flip
A daydream into a night,
One that would cross no matter what –
Aspire.

Inevitable Loss

A falling night takes over the smile;
I wait for the night to end,
Yet I never find a sun.
Deep inside, an old truth persists –
My child never grew up,
And my longstanding man is still standing up.
Time attempts to weep light.
I question, what will happen now?
Ones will die, an infinite inevitable lie.
Hence they won't want to open their eyes,
Flowers will age and fall apart.
The long-awaited sun won't find eyes,
No matter how bright outside,
Darkness prevails from the inside.
Screams may call for ones that could be alive;
We will have to face it, no one will survive.
We will call one another, but are there others?
I will ask myself, have I persisted or left apart?
The answer does not matter as –
I seem to be hollow in a world –
That confused life with death,
And children with old-aged.
Silence is what we own –
God, do you listen to this silence?
Horrible as it may seem, peaceful you are.
Enlighten us.

Rush of Pain

I saw the sun,
And I started to run.
I thought it was there.
When I arrived –
It disappeared.
Dark appeared;
I screamed.
Fear of not being heard –
Kept calling the loneliness in me.
It takes me to where I am –
A place that fills me with guilt.
It forces me to submit myself –
Life drops out of my eyes,
Unlike my sky, they were not dry.
Ones that turn wet and generously –
Hold on to this life.
They did not stop,
We had to survive.
Pain was testing me,
And I was not willing to fail myself.
Go on.

Mind My Fight

A night of falling stars,
Couldn't realize if I was awakened
Or if it was my night.
Deep and far –
Dust of gold showed up.
It made smiles above in my skies –
The Lord asked about my
Other I
Cold wind blew me out –
Pushed on the ground
Storming light.
Got me to open my eyes
It read, "Reveal yourself."
Hollow I was –
It calmed down.
Why?
You are a thought in your mind.
One spirited line.
Do not fight your own one.
If they fight you,
You are within your mind.
It cannot hurt –
Unless you surrender yourself.
Get them out of you,
Let it storm –
Attempting to frighten you.
Walk the way you want,
Rule your path now –
Or give your light out.

Deep Breath

Time rushed my feet.
I was ignoring the night
And trying to keep the light.
For a while, I even felt the sun –
For another, I couldn't breathe at all.
I couldn't tell,
Was it day or night?
My eyes were faking my sight.
Trust is hard, even to my own eyes.
I got to question everything around.
Are the stars really pretty that much?
They were never beautiful enough.
Unique but not new –
Dreams end, and mornings come.
I will resist whatever arrives –
Fight my world non-stop.
Then, the rain comes.
It drops everywhere,
So you can't hide.
It is in my head –
I can lie,
So I close my eyes,
I remember and then run.
Go somewhere along the sun –
But why does darkness have to be sad?
We can't even live along –
The fear of our own selves.
Question as you like –
Fate manipulates my faith;
Heavy thoughts that want to reside.
It is the one time when –
Loneliness is what I want –
But life wants your love;
It is tiring,
I don't want to open my eyes.
I won't see the light
Even if I am bright.
I will walk away,
But life is everywhere.
I do not return to fight –
But to beat life and prove a light.

I may lose a round,
But many wars to come.
I can succeed;
I was born to draw this line.

Flash Run

I was lost in the mirror,
Me had left my I –
And I stayed alone somewhere far.
Darkness threw me away,
And the fear called me in nearby.
I was found trying to breathe,
But deep inside there was no beat.
Happiness joined others,
And my sadness was bright.
Calling for mercy upon the heart;
I was running to quit my sky.
Dreams just died,
And the future had arrived.
I wasn't there –
But I was observing it all;
Like a film without a hero –
But you still enjoy the run.
Felt like I wanted to get revenge,
I could fake it all:
I could become him,
One who'd never have an I.

Loud

He was depth,
But the music always
Played his mind.
Loud, it used to take him
For heights.
He was afraid to look down.
He could not continue to crawl,
He used to sneak down –
Away from the peak
Not rationalizing
Following his beat –
The morning comes,
And he is yet to sleep.
Dimming his eyes, not –
The darker it gets,
The more he craves to see it all.
The limitation was in his mind –
And that beat did not stop.
Thinking about his path–
He knew that the show was yet to start.
Silent world in a loud mind,
It makes the journey worthwhile.
Find the depth in you,
It can make you fly.

Unjust

I have not known power,
But I have had strength.
My limits were the boundaries
Of the universe, and the universe
Is a point in time. Who owns time?
Eternity is captivated
By its own infinity;
Past is free and the future seems anxious;
It is waiting for time
When now it becomes.
Now is the power.
We reimagine to satisfy our need;
Those illusions are
What we strive to see,
Words we force to hear.
Ideas cross the mind –
At a lighting speed,
Craving for darkness
So they can shine and breed.
These non-sense feelings,
Fill them up with nostalgic dreams.
Drug your night, and it could bring
You the past indeed.
Come back to when
You were first on one path,
You must have been
Behind some other place.
Haven't you missed
Someone back far?
Even no one could
Become someone, sometimes.
Annoying as it feels,
It was made unjust.
It is naturally not right.
Diagonal minds don't cross,
Two ones can align.
It takes a bit of energy to start up,
Then you will need to run a story
To an end.
Think, dream on.

Home

I knocked on my door,
It never opened up.
My home is no longer mine –
So I walk down the stairs,
Slowly I disappear
To my own self.
Time is changing,
It is becoming fast.
It makes me slow,
And I used to leave for nights.
Now my dreams are trapped –
Dare to make those come true,
And reality becomes
All what you've got.
Priceless as it seems,
Truth is rather a reflection
Of what we only believe as right.
What is wrong son?
You always wanted to grow up.
Here you are,
Walking among the old ones.
This innocence deep inside –
Became a memorable smile.
At war, only dead ones
Appreciate peace of mind.
Fly, there will soon be
No place for you in the sky.
This is the era of stars.
Everyone has to shine, fight.

Fit to Life

The world packed my
Life inside a box;
It was a white one.
Sneak a peek
To unleash the black;
And I will show you
A harmonic contrast.
The reflection is real.
Opposite sounds
That eliminate one another –
Silence in the middle of the mass.
Just you –
The center of your
Crowded mind.
Busy beats striking your head;
Endless directions;
Nowhere have you wanted to be.
Claim someone you are not.
Beg to flee –
Make the wish,
Follow your path.
Turn back –
Blow a dream.

Flee, Free, Flee

Victory was uncertain,
The battle was over,
Fighters were down,
Majority surrendered,
Either for peace or out of fear.
No one went back home.
Victorious is a free man.
Free in an empty land,
Ruled by blood and death.
Free was lonely;
Moreover free is alone.
Beauty turning ugly.
Relativity matters, no more.
Less is a bless.
Wind tells a story –
Of victorious the free.
One that did never exist;
Illusionist rather than realistic,
Closer to a dream,
More than what it seems.
Flee, free, flee.

Comeback

I seemed unfit.
My clock simply missed.
My time has passed,
And I drilled into the past.
I went somewhere I am not,
Foreign to my mind –
Somehow,
Still able to figure it out.
Thinking about who I am –
Following the passion
That I've got;
This deep spark inside –
It opts to get out.
Show the world a flame,
Enright something
That could be strong,
Bold my fingerprint,
Make it become a trace,
Bring the roots back on track
It has been shadowed for long –
Now I am returning.
Give me the light that I am.

Mountains

I was waiting for the wind;
But I had rain.
The storm persists,
And the garden degrades.
My roof is closing in,
And the sky is becoming far.
Cloud wanting to tick out –
So stars hide.
Just like every other night,
My I arrives and my
Twinkles check out.
Scarce men, yes they are –
Loneliness killed them all,
Yet it kept me alive.
Faith goes along with patience,
And I want to step back though
To where the top comes down –
So it picks me up, and
I scream to echo myself up again.
Take me down time,
To the bottom of the valley
Where I shall be.
No stars will find me –
Words will fill the space,
And it is where the wind hides.
It will carry my papers up –
Somewhere really high.
Shattered into millions of pieces
To fill the sky –
Freedom is just fine.

Stairs to the Sky

Smiles come to meet my eyes,
And my eyes refuse the sun.
The moon wants to shine,
And I cannot get alive.
Broken heart is all what I got.
My fingers try to create words,
Yet useless life becomes
The truth lies behind lies,
And only the innocent dies.
Those liars get alive,
Pure hearts fade,
And only deception survives.
Fake the night becomes,
And Illusions these stars really are.
We refuse to admit but
The 'lonely' truth is a Lie.
People push me to smile.
While my eyes are indeed mild
And the soul is tearing wild,
They ask me to get out –
And I tell them,
Why don't you
Come down –
Past is eternal
Visit me and get alive.

Lost Child

Three minutes never passed,
And hours just left.
I stayed alone with seconds
That kept refusing to go away.
They were counting down,
And refused to fade up.
I cried,
But tears were going inside.
Screams were all loud,
But none of them were mine.
My words jumped
Into letters in dark.
An amazing smile
Enlightens a lie,
And the sun did not
Want to share light.
The stars are to weep the sky.
The moon is tired
Of being up in the dark.
The mother keeps calling
Her lost son,
And the kid who was born a man –
Did never become a child.
It appears sad but never real.
An illusion refuses to leave.
Only the walker persists to stay;
Not alive but fixed alone in a path
Even darkness refused
To adopt a black heart,
And so I couldn't breathe,
I wanted to leave.
Where shall I run?
Death is everywhere,
Yet it does not want
To take me away.
Life wants to end this path
Continuity means eternity,
And I crave to fall.
Destiny is not fair,
But it may take us to the end.
During lost seconds I was found;

Shall I cry? Or give it a real smile?
In the end,
I will simply close my eyes.

Gone

As my ink becomes dry,
Speechless,
But I persist to talk.
My pen is still writing.
No one wants
To fill the blanks,
And because of my tearful words,
Miserable all my stories are,
Even when we all smile,
Each story is a chapter,
And my chapters fell apart.
In a book that refused
To be priced,
Words are to reach the world,
And I will remain in the corner,
Begging my words
Not to leave me alone.
Selfish, that's who I am,
I refuse to give my papers.
I'm dictating the pen
To remain in the hand.
I hurry to hide my papers
From light.
They want to see my words.
I ran away from all of them
To this warm corner far.
Here, I'll speak through dry ink.
I'll hide my papers from light
Even when it's night,
And I'll master myself
As alone

ANOTHER I

SHADY HALLAB

INDEX